# A GATHERING

*of some of my New Mexico Poems*

# A GATHERING

## of some of my New Mexico Poems

by Victor di Suvero

with an Introduction by Orlando Romero

PENNYWHISTLE PRESS

Santa Fe, New Mexico

**Previous Works:**

*Salt and the Heart's Horizons*
*Sight Poems*
*San Francisco Poems*
*The Net & Other Poems*
*Tesuque Poems*
*naked Heart*
*Harvest Time*
*Spring Again*
*Moving On*

**Editor:**

*¡Saludos!*
*The Bilingual Anthology*
*of the Poetry of New Mexico*
*Sextet*
*We Came to Santa Fe*

Design/Production: SunFlower Designs of Santa Fe

Front Cover Photo: Barbara Windom

Back Cover Photo: Dana Walton

**Library of Congress Control Number:**
2009941361
ISBN: 978–0–938631–51–4   paper

PUBLISHED BY

PENNYWHISTLE PRESS
PO Box 734, Tesuque, NM 87574 USA

*Para todos nosotros —*

*For all of us —*

# Contents

# Introduction
## by Orlando Romero

This collection of poems by Victor di Suvero takes place in a very ancient land and are told by a man with the soul of the ancients and the passion of a young man. Grandfather would say that the ancient cottonwoods whose brilliant green would announce our birth in Spring and their shimmering golden Fall colors would announce our respite were the only true wise voices in this land because they had lived for centuries. They had witnessed the proud, haughty, poor, the blind and those who had seen for the very first time.

This land is like no other. Yes, there is Tuscany, Provence and the wildest of places in Argentina, Russia, Nepal and far more exotic destinations. Yet just one calm morning in late Spring when everything is in bloom or just one warm afternoon in the late Fall that brings both the *viejos y los jovenes* to sit together in La Resolana in this place of four vivid, Vivaldi seasons can be like no other. Di Suvero's pen captures it, brings it to life, sometimes dissects it, but then gently, lovingly puts it back together again in the symmetry and order of the poet.

Di Suvero, like all good poets, makes you think about how we live our lives or, more precisely, how time and events slip through our fingers and we seem totally unable to control our destinies. Yet, precisely because of that, it is the time that becomes so precious, illusive yet to be savored, celebrated, commemorated.

This land that he has encountered with its ghosts of ancient Indians, Spanish settlers, mayordomos and parciantes and the daily lives of his neighbors are not fiction but realities waiting for the poet to chronicle them, at times revealing hidden shadows, exposing his own heart's wanderings, questions, frailties and fears.

Poetry is not for fools, yet they are the most in need of it. Poetry is not for the rich, no book can hold or dispense the words of the wise. Politicians do not need poetry. There is no perceived power in poetry; yet I've seen a few stanzas bring tears to the most powerful of men. Di Suvero's poetry has a little of everything for every man or everyone. It's that small amount that just might get us through.

## How Did We Come Here?

How did we come here and to what end?
What was it that drew us here?
Was it the land calling, the piñon?
The great shaped clouds blessing the blue of the sky?
Was it the dawn's quiet or the other one,
The one that comes after the day of work, at dusk
In summer, promising rest and respite and all
The other good things we dreamed of when we let
       ourselves do so?

How did we come here? Was it the wind?
Or was it the star that moved us, all of us?
Tell me about the Anasazi, how they came here,
Out of the Earth's navel, the Sipapu, the hole
In the ground made by Coyote when Lightning
Came after him — tell me about the Old Ones,
The ones who came from over the edge
By starlight, riding the wind, driven
By hope as well as by terror — tell me!

How is it that we came here, to this place
Where the cottonwood grows? We brought
Our cooking pots and histories and prayers,
We brought our hopes to make a place
Where the children's children not yet
Born may come to tell each other stories
Of how it is that we came here
And why — and they may end up
Knowing more about it than we do now.
I have come to give
Thanks to wind and star and call of land
And all that served
To bring us here.

## For All of Us

This was the sea once and I walk across the hills,
Down to the arroyo and up again with my eyes
Swimming across the face of a blind escarpment,
Seeing red and ochre bluffs as some strange
Finned creature must have eyed them
When all was water here instead of air and
Another way of being was the way.

I think of that reptilian ancestor whose appetite
For light drove him and his kind to breathe air,
Instead of water. They took possession of the
Land wondering if there was another way to be.

I know that when my children first saw the light
They came out of that same sea and their children
Too, in turn, will rise from there into the air
With perhaps a better chance of finding still
Another way.

This was the sea once and the sun rests on solstice
Night while the midsummer dark is forked
By lightning that charges down the draw,
Driving the huge and crackling thunder into the
Ground reminding us once more that all things
Change, some slowly, and others in a flash.
Always another way to be.

## In The Early Spring

Imagine the work the roots do when
The ground thaws and the radicle begins
To swell and the rootlets go out first as hair
Thin explorations, then filling out while in
The dark, growing with no air but purpose,
With no light but the need to feed the plant
Above that will flower in the sun in time.

The work the roots do is silent — it
Generates no appreciation or applause. The
Roots serve and feed the plant they are a
Part of — and the flowering becomes seed,
Which falls into the ground to round the
Cycle once again with light into another
Time, another growing, serving the entirety,
Silent as the stretch of time.

I see my children going out into the world
Raising their wings into the air as I pray the
Wind to ease their landings here on an earth
Carpeted with grass and flowers all of which
Would not be there without the work that
The roots have done.

## We Do Not Own

You don't own the four directions child,
They own you. The mountain owns you.
The meadows by the river, fringed and tasseled
By the cottonwoods, own you. The bluffs
In the barrancas you see when you look north,
Own you. Even the arroyo owns you.
You, child, are theirs. You belong to them.

Someone, somewhere, that first day of fences
Said "mine" and said "for my children,"
And then it grew and grew and counties
Became states and became nations
And Cain and Abel's story kept on being
Taught because it made us righteous
In the land—that's really where it all began.

First slings, then bows and arrows
And then the guns—until we broke the
Atom up to make sure no one else could
Or would find a way to breach our walls,
Still forgetting we do not own a thing.

Child, the deer knows the way, so does Coyote.
They know where the seasons take them;
They know where the wind comes from
And where it goes. Even Raven plays
Those currents in the air we cannot see.  ↳

And yet each one of them knows home —
The matted corner in the meadow, the den
Scooped out of sandstone cliff, the dark
Nests in the arms of trees all say
This is the place of rest for them.

Taste all the distances you need, explore
The gorges, discover roadways made of dreams,
But be ready when the time comes, to say
This is the place in which to rest
The place to be, knowing you will not
Ever own it if you count on staying free.

## In the Fall

Now the leaves give their color back
To the sun.
                        They dance their golden
Flickering while celebrating all the work
The days have made out of air and earth, and
Out of water and of time.
                        We choose to stand
Here knowing that what we have done is to
Serve in an exercise of stewardship.
                        And yet
We did go out into the world and learned to deal
With one another; learning also how to bring
The harvest in and to share and teach while
Still continuing to learn.
                        We've done all that
Which we have done so as to realize that
This season is a shining thing, alive
With fire, endowed with smiles and not
A fading piece of tired remembering.

The sun's light is in a trillion leaves
Each one dancing its gold back
To where it came from
Reminding us with every motion that
What we have enjoyed is still with us
Not only in memory, but in our blood
And skin, bringing us into the dance
Of knowing who and how well we are and
What we've managed to get done while here.

## Time is All We Have

Time is all we have, to give, to use,
To share with the beloved, time is all
We have — given to us as long
As body's strength permits us life —
All else does not belong to us —
Stewards of one kind or another,
Caretakers or wastrels, good ones,
Bad ones and some in between,
Solitary, gregarious, committed
To a cause or to acquisitions,
We share this passage we call time
While doing all the other things we do.

We sleep, sing, dance and work, bring
Children into the world while killing
Enemies as well as animals and birds.
With each and every act of ours we take
Pieces of our capital without remorse.
Every single thing takes time — sleep
Takes time, stupidity as well — the one
Argument for the good life is economy
Achieved by not wasting time on guilts,
Regrets or even penances.

                                    Time's faces,
The dark one and the light, are the faces
Of our lives — sad and somber,
Serious and wondrous, bright and full
Laughter from one moment to another
When we notice them reflected
In the mirrors of our time
As we move along our voyages
And smile.

## Time Teaches

Time teaches us to serve the arts
As acolytes are trained. Some of us
Simply remain there, in training,
Raising money, sending newsletters out
Into the world, forgetting to graduate,
Forgetting the one point of it,
The joy of being and of
This world we can enjoy with smiles.

It's all here in this high desert:
A daughter's wedding coming in the Fall,
The sound of hooves drumming on the wind,
The wry smile of a friend dead too soon of AIDS,
The working dreams of a new house,
While politicians play their shabby games;
The winds of friendship are serene and good and
Even Othello Simpson's looming presence on CNN
Does not undo our sense of right
As the Spring's first crocus springs into the hands of lovers
And children run to play —   ↪

                    Learning
A piece of music can teach us how to hear
The cantata of the streets, the odes of clouds
And the songs immanent in the voice
Of the beloved.

                    It is Cordelia's speech
To her Dad, sweet, impossible and mad
Old Lear. It is her kiss upon his cheek
That heals the King.

                    Poetry does serve all
Of us—even as the seasons and the horses do—
As lovers serve each other in the night of days
And in the day of nights while time
Teaches us to serve as we go along our ways.

## Sunday Afternoon

Leaving the Valley, crossing the Rio Grande,
Heading south into the high mountains
Leaving Okeh Owingeh behind, crossing over
Into the Pueblos of Santa Clara and San Ildefonso
With their ancient histories, their autumn fields
Harvested golden gray against the earth,
Heading up into the ancient walls of red rock
The road winding alongside fissures as it rises
Above the villages below heading up into
Buttresses that seem as if they had been built
By giants in other times, ancient rocks
Overtowering the valleys below that had been
There for aeons while mere humans
Below had scratched out livings, learned
To make pots and invented ways of being
With their gods, heavens and after lives.

Suddenly turning into Valle Caldera where
A million years ago a volcanic eruption
Had created an open space, wide, golden,
That had become grassland over the years
Contrasting again with the Castlements,
Towers of red rock that continue rising
Silently, as from the time of creation, still
Heading up towards Jemez, the oldest Pueblo
Still closed since the time of the Pueblo Revolt
The only time the Conquistadors were ever
Thrown back out of any area of this continent. ↪

Then, still rising up the gradient to the
So called "Hill" — Los Alamos — birthplace of this Atomic age
Driving by Oppenheimer Road, Bikini Street and even
      Fermi Avenue,
Fermi's wife having been my father's cousin, suddenly turning
Geologic past, atomic present and familial connections with
The trip through the Anasazi, the "ones who came before,"
The early Puebloan Cultures, Oñate, de Vargas, Peralta,
Then Kit Carson, Kearney, the Bankers and Looters,
Up to the time when the country needed a place
Out of the way, secret fastness, blocked entrances
To build the weapons that could win a war
And then also blow the planet to smithereens
Making a blast
Of sound in the middle of my head that still
Reverberates.

          And then, going through the canyons beyond
The zones labeled "Security" and "Area 43" I was back
Into the landscape with its great red rocks breathing
A sigh as the Jemez timberland begins to stretch
Almost as if it were waking into the calm that comes
After storms had lashed the consciousness and find
My way to the Tribal Fair, the Visitor Center, the
Gallery and the friend's paintings living only in the moment,
For the moment, before even thinking about the return.

Constrants, juxtapositions, ancient ways presented
In new framings, traditions turned into artifacts,
All the ways of living with, as opposed to dying alone.
Beauty captured by the artist's hand and eye
To be shared with others crowding the area, ↳

The timelessness of beauty, of being alive
Become the teaching.
                              Then to begin to return.
Dante's ascension through the three worlds of his belief
Were a one-way trip while I faced the necessity
Of retracing steps, going back through history as night
Began its quick approach.
                              At this point all I could
Think of was getting back and would I find my way.

Easy I thought, having been through it once, but fate
Or chance caught me short in Los Alamos again and
I found myself at dusk trying to determine
How to extricate myself from the entanglements
Of "Areas 45" and "521" and Lawrence Drive and
DANGER with its Radioactive signs beside the small
Museum in which the evolution of the possibility
That we might eventually succeed in blowing up
The future is pleasantly presented, I hear.

But I did find my way out of that dark wood, out
Of the dark canyons that surrounded it, to eventually
Drive down to the San Ildefonso and Santa Clara fields
And then to find my way back to the road that led
To the place where this trip had started realizing once
And once again that it's not only the going but also
The coming back that defines one's world, one's dreams
And those of all with whom we are enlivened.

# Ulysses in Tesuque

On that shore far away
After the ring of blood
Had been filled and after
The other shades had come and gone
It was Tiresias
Who told me I would find
Peace and rest in the mountains—
If I were to go inland so far, he said,
That a wayfarer I would meet
Would ask the use of the oar
I would be carrying on my shoulder.
"Would that be a winnowing flail?"
He'd ask, and then I'd set it down,
Make my sacrifice to Poseidon,
And find my peace at last—

And I did that—and I did plant
My oar here and built a house—
But the grapes of my desire
Were not made into wine
And the roses in the garden
Are beaten down by summer hail
While dreams of soft sand,
Salt spume and sea shells merge
With the talk of old compañeros
Remembering all the voyages
And the long way home.

All those things consume my nights
And eat the marrow of the years
I've left to breathe—not knowing
If the thunder roars to send me on,
Back to the sea or to keep me here
Until that night that has no dawn
Comes with its mirror to find me out.

# In Every Dream of Heaven

In every dream of Heaven
There is always that great light
And that wanting to go there —
Always toward the light —
Even the seed in the dirt pushes
Up into the light and air —

Coyote's pups crawl out of
Their burrow, out into the world
To move into their light, and
Ours, where we can be at one
With the sun and where even
At night the stars and all
The other suns come out
For all to see and to be with.

From Ahknaton on
The Light and the
Idea of God have been one.

Dante's vision and the stars
Still blaze here tonight while
I fumble, looking for a match.

## There, Out of the Dark

There, there from the cloud's edge, out of the dark;
Light, as in lightning, cutting through dark, there,
Over there, from out of the mountain's side, a bite
Of it, a flash, cutting into the body of this dark, this
Dark time—and over there, on the other, the far
Side, another flash, skimming through, piercing its
Way to dispel and unseat this dark that has been
Wrapping itself around the various elements that
Matter in our lives.
                    Not enough for us to say "We can manage,"
Or "We made it through before, we can do it." Not enough
To claim the comfort of the dark, or believing it's easier
Not to know the Wheres and the Whys or even the
With Whoms.
               We have become a sorry lot in this dark,
Lacking even the arrogance of Lucifer who chose that
Which is forever dark out of the brilliance,
                          And in the dark
There are those who will say it is not Poetry's role to play
Upon the way people are governed or managed but I
Say that Poetry is too valuable a trust to be sent
Skulking into corners where there is no light.

I hear a call for people everywhere
To move together with all others of kind heart
Into the light of day, willing to share words
With smiles in all those ways that will put
Darkness where it belongs, away, away, away.

## That Night in Bethlehem

There she was in the snow, teenager,"
Pregnant, about to have her water break,
Engaged, not even married to that older
Sweet man Joseph, good friend of her mother
Anna. He had said all right, angels
And all that talk, with no idea at all
Of what he had let himself in for.

                       And
She, whose name would in time become
Repeated more than the name of any,
Any other woman, Mary, Maria, she,
Scared, black hair long in the snow, not
Like the bleached blond version of the
Virgin they would make of her, with
Her breasts swelling and her water
Breaking, pushing, on the straw, covered
Only with her cloak and the donkey's ragged
Blanket, not thinking, just pushing
And so involved that if the angels
Were indeed there, and Gloria in Excelsis,
She was not aware of anything except
Her baby, the one they would all call
"Fruit of her womb."      ↪

                    But the blood,
The water, the warm water finally
From the kitchen upstairs, tired, baby
Finally to breast, to sleep with no
Absolutely no, idea, that all of this cold
Night, after the shepherds and the blessings
The Angels and the Gloria in Excelsis
After the coming of the Three Kings
Would eventually turn into murder of her
Child on the criminal's cross and that
Her body, having been used to make
A child, would never be allowed
To be seen, to breathe air, to become
A full figured woman except on
The canvases of painters yet to come
In strange parts of the world who
Would adopt her, change her image
A thousand ways from Sunday,
This Winter Sunday, the one of the
Sagrada Familia made up of
The carpenter, the scared teenager with
The long black hair and the Son of God,
We pray, wondering what the story
Really was, before it was changed
And made into so many, many
Religions that all join together
To Celebrate this Christmas time.

# This Night a Child is Born

In Tesuque, on Christmas eve
Before midnight, at the church
In the Pueblo, where all the pews
Have been taken out and stacked
In the snow, the dancers come
As the bell rings to call
All of us to celebrate
The miracle—"A child is
born to us." The angels sing
And the dancers come
In perfect rows
And the Spirit
Is indeed with them
And with us
As the Buffalo is praised
With branches of piñon and
Branches of juniper
And deer
Walk among us and tears
Well up and we know the kings
Will come and bring gold and
Frankincense and myrrh but
This night we have all brought
Ourselves to give to Him again as
The drum beats and the snow falls.

## Way To Be

Servants, to serve, not observe,
To preserve, not destroy, serving.

Not making rules for others, not
Dictating behavior but guiding,
Helping along the way, making
Things easier, the climb less steep.

Celebrating; smiling, not scowling.
In the right, not righteous, being,
Not telling. Leaving judgement to judges,
Commitments only made voluntarily,
Forgetting force or fear, letting the
Threat of fire forever after flow
Out into a river of mercy and drown,
With compassion overriding conceit.

Making sure that one will continue
To serve, preserving and working,
To make certain that each one
Of us will learn how to be gentle
Even while stupidity and greed
Slaver at the gates.
                              We will
Continue to be engaged in all that
Which turns seed into flower
Serving the light.

## Moving From Tesuque

Uproot, deracinate, relocate, start over,
Cast off—all those words indicate
Change, mobility, moving on once more,
Making camp for one night or for a few.

How sedentary we've become!

Surely strange when all our pasts
Were all essentially nomadic.

The society works toward stability
Seducing even the wanderer by
Making it easier to stay than to go.

We've become creatures of comforts,
Attached to the trees we've planted,
To the sunsets we've seen move
From there to there as seasons
Came and went, praying constantly
For the right of staying in that
One place called home and now,
Having to go on once more,
I am reminded that wandering
Is our fate and that permanence
Is delusion.

So long as we have
Feet and eyes and hopes to move us
We go before the long night comes.

# Arriving in Taos

After going north
Through the intensities of color with
Sky blue so blue, cottonwoods turning, brilliant
Chamisa, asters, gold, purple, the sweep when suddenly
Rounding and rising with the road into the vista
Of distances, Blue Mountain, the cut of the canyon
In the middle, the crisp of the air we could taste
Getting finally into the intensity of traffic and
Pulling over into the parking lot before the shapes
At the back of the one and only Church of St. Francis
So far from Assisi yet as significant and then
To be confronted by the "Two Graces," a shop
Where we were offered and indeed bought
Two lives in the shape of two good books,
Frank Waters, whom I had known
And D.H. Lawrence whose work I had known,
Making those two Taoseños alive again for me,
Bringing me back some forty years when
I had first discovered this corner
Of the world — and all that time
Returned in a rush with all those memorable ones,
Jaime de Angulo, Wells, Huxley, all the Indians and
Those others, Mabel, Merwin, Brett, O'Keefe,
Bill Collier, Thornton Wilder and the Greek
Who owned La Fonda with Lawrence's
Forbidden paintings, all of them there
Along with Frieda, Fechin and Millicent Rogers
Whom I had met or come to know through
What they had done and left for us
All that time ago. Two books evoking
So many lives and teachings, even
Manby's cottonwoods or what's left
Of them along the road — all turning
Into a piece of my past while still
Moving forward, moving on.

## At La Villita

In this place of quiet, by the river, green,
A thousand miles from the nearest sea
Where kind and gentle care kept him
From dying as so many of his like had done
Out of drink, despair, betrayals and even war
Where he was comforted in spite of ways
Which were not the ones he had been born
To live; he found himself repeatedly facing
The surge of ocean in dreams, in visions
Along with the grace of gulls and dolphins
As he learned to live a life with horses,
Eagles, coyotes and with cats and dogs along
With mountain men and women who had
Never even seen the sea but had heard of it.

Blending trust with gratitude, he would
Find ways from time to time to taste
The salt air at dawn, hear the wave's slap
And flinch once more as the wind at the bow
Would burn his face and eyes on lookout.

It was not his youth he wanted back, not
The ability to move with sea bag upon shoulder
Down to shipping hall and the unknown beyond
But the sea itself that covers so much
More than half of our planet's skin that kept
Calling him back to that Republic of Ocean
In which the Sacred Islands shape hearts
And feelings without boundaries, without signs
That proclaim "Private Property — Do Not Enter."

We all were born in that sea which filled
Our mothers' wombs before we came out
To breathe air as we have learned to do  ↘

Among all the other things we've learned;
And so many of us seem to be inured
To the sea's call, to its demands and disciplines
That we forget that place we all came from
Which is still our destination even though
So many of us live in mountain meadows.

                                        We
Rush through city streets and continue to engage
Our lives in growing crops, in doing business and
Driving ourselves and others down the freeways
While going about the work of wars of one kind
Or another in the names of Liberty and Peace.

The tides still rise and fall in daily certainty
And the whales and dolphins still breathe air
After having gone back to the sea after their time
As mammals on these lands, and now, with
The Global Warming of this small planet on which
We live he wonders how long before the sea
Will come once again to claim its shores.

                                  He knows
It will not be long after he will have gone, and
Still it amuses him to think how much more
In the way of violence takes place on land
Than in the stretches of the Ocean that his kind
Has always known to be the better place to be.

That place of long horizons and dreams
Where one can be one with one another and
With the stars, their constellations, their ways
And the thousand million nebulae that are the Universe
So that we may eventually learn to know the wellness
That winds and dark ocean depths can give to us.

# The Cemetery at La Villita

A friend's sister is buried
In the family plot, in the cemetery
Tucked in the grove of cottonwoods
Around which our fields grow
Their alfalfa, their corn, their other
Fruits and vegetables.

                       As we have come
To live with others, in villages, in cities,
Does that mean we should be laid
To rest with others of our kind?

                              It seems
It's been a human desire to be together
Not only when we walk and talk and
Go to circuses or parades but even
When we die so that we can be
Together.

                A thousand people come
To mourn this daughter, sister,
Mother, friend and after the ritual
They all disperse as the autumn wind
Had claimed its own once more.

# Tripping

Up the Valley once more, up to Taos
So many times over the years before
But not golden glorious as this time
Going out of the canyon into the gold.

The cottonwoods giving their glories
Back to the sun and its bright light
That light that had given them life in the Spring
And the great light of summer now just gone.

Each season sets it mark on this land
Each year its tiny fraction of the infinite
Each moment quivering in the soft wind
As each golden leaf gives us its life this day.

And then coming back down the next afternoon.
With the impeccable colors still holding
Their own in our eyes the darker green
Of the pines framing the world and its look.

Realizing once again that each moment we see
Is both singular and yet food for eternity
While we keep barreling through our duties
And the daily grind without stopping enough
To see the colors of the golden moments nor
To hear the sound of the world turning.

The gold shimmers as we drive through it
Knowing it was all that came before
That made this day, this light possible.

## *Autumn Leaves*

The golden leaves falling from the cottonwoods
Make a carpet around the last brave roses
That have managed to keep some color
Of their own in their red and orange petals
That survived the first frosts of the year.

The richness of the remaining green
With all the autumn colors sing a song
Of summer memories and of cold to come.

A time of beauty that is both a time
Of loss and of new promises.
                          We are
Fortunate to be the point between
The past and all
That is still to come.


Summer's gone, Autumn's here
Harvest time before cold Winter
Comes down to the fields.
                          Stillness
In the air. The world is waiting
And all that has to be done
Is being done one day at a time.


The leaves give the sun back
Its color as they fall golden
To the ground.
                    The trees know
That in the Spring there will
Be new ones to bring green
Back into the light before
We will see their gold again.  ↪

A pigeon came to sit on the head of St. Francis
There, the statue on the west side of the garden.
They both seemed to smile for a moment
Then the bird had other things to do
And left and it really seemed that St. Francis
Turned his head up and to the left
For just a moment.
                              Then the wind came up,
A few more leaves fluttered down the golden day
And all went back to be just as it had been before.


It really depends on the yardstick
That is used to determine the length
Of anything, a smile, a life, some silk
Or even cotton, a marriage and even
An absence.
                    Choose your own carefully
Before determining the length of anything.


In a country run by thieves the rich
Are honored, cared for, protected
Because, if not, there would be
Not much left to steal.
                              This runs so
Long as things don't get too much
Out of hand.

## Winter Cold Again

Cold this morning, cold this winter day,
Snow, ice and wind from the mountains
Conspire to make us truly grateful
That we have been fortunate enough
To build a shelter that guards us all
From this unusual cold.

At the same time, dreaming of the warmth
Of sand upon the beaches, the littorals
Of tropic seas, knowing that in these days
It is not impossible to exchange seasons
With an airline ticket or to purchase visits
To the earthly paradise we choose to choose
With smiles.

But the cold reminds us
That the planning had to have been there.
The firewood stacked, the store rooms
Filled, the blankets readied and the food
Stored carefully so that one could indeed count
On weathering the winter.

Meanwhile
The dreams of Spring find their way
Through the walls, the roof and into doors
And windows, and because of them, we can
Look forward into a time that is easier
Than the one we're faced with in these
Mornings that are so cold the air itself
Becomes as brittle as the sheets of ice
That slide down from the roof
And crack, reminding us
That if we wake at all
We'll have another chance.

## Beyond the Pass

It is truly wonderful
How we go on without thinking
Until death, divorce or war —
One of the great severances —
Comes along and demands that the ledgers
Be audited, examined,
So as to see that the various entries
Tally with the end result which brought
The self to its present pass.

Some of us stop there,
At the pass, and,
Cozened by the very newness of thought
Find ourselves buried in an avalanche
Of snowy reflections
Or frozen by the wind of recriminations;

And we forget that beyond the pass
Lie the rich countries
Burgeoning green in watered valleys,
Which can only be reached
By bringing heart and motion to bear.

## Chimayo

Most of us are just that—pilgrims, wandering
From place to place, to find one more holy than another,
A piece of earth where heart and hope could find
Some ease, some sense of having come home, or rest,
In spirit—a place which would confer a blessing
Upon our lives—whether that wanderer be Muslim
On his Hadj, Catholic on his way to Lourdes or
Of any other faith that would bring him or her to
The Ganges River's bank or the Santuario at Chimayo.

This last one perhaps can tell more stories than any other
Since it is tied to the belief that it is the earth itself
That is the essence of the miracle—the planet's self
Through which one can run one's hand and feel all
That's been felt by those who came before as they did
Before it came to be part of the Catholic tradition of
Today.

            Before, when the Indians had found
This earth, this dust that we all are, to be totally
Different, to be sacred, to be an enabling agent
Making those who came to it become the better
Portion of their own selves, this matter of belief
Tended by a sacristan who came himself from
Far away, responsible to maintain belief
No matter how great the journey or how angry and
Desperate the need—the pilgrim's shell, the staff,
The crutches hung up there in the rafters and
All the rest of the paraphernalia of belief where they
Are tended gently even though we all come to know
We carry the solace in our own hearts and only
Sometimes need company for the journey as we go
Which is why pilgrims do seem to travel
Better when they go with each other
To find the solace they all seek.

## Not Dreaming

It came out of the kiva
And danced that night —
Naked but for the deer belt;

Became the buck, startled,
Chased through brush
*Reaching* the high prairie —
Hooves *drumming, going*
The sound *sustaining* it,
Air *rushing, going, getting* away,
Down by the river
Through the cottonwoods:
More trail, more scent
More piñon,
Back up to the mesa
Hooves *drumming*
*Going, going*
Through the piñon
Fast, *going,*
Lungs *heaving,*
*Stopping* finally
Alone under the stars;
Lungs *heaving,*
Pink foam at the nostrils —

Great gasps
*Devouring* the air
*Trembling*
Legs *twitching,*
*Standing, twitching,*
*Stopping, waiting,*
Until after one huge breath
My heart suddenly
Slowed
And walked back to the house
And knew where it had been.
And we held each other
Until day broke.

## On the Way

These ancient mountain passes with
Red stone rearing up and over the road,
Loom over the traveler, warning
That this land is sacred and open
Only to the pilgrim with an open heart.

All that came before and all that is to come
Are joined in each of the pilgrim's steps
As he moves out into the world of light.

He brings memories and disciplines with him.
The times when he would sit to reach
The unreachable, when he would kneel
To offer his pledges and his prayers, when
He would bow and clap his hands and
Sing with a choir of others just like him
Looking for the answers in rituals, in
Prayers and chants, always one step
Away from the one place he always
Was looking for.

              So, now, out of the canyon,
Stepping into the light, having discovered
That over that hill to the West was a temple
Where a famous teacher was known to come
He thought for a moment once again that
All he had learned and had come to know
Would finally lead him to the very heart
Of the world he wanted. ⤵

                    At that moment
He looked out at a branch almost within
Reach and saw a piece of the sky come down
Settling its blue into the form of a bird
Where it stayed for an instant looking
At him and then flew up and out
And became once again part of the sky.

Bird and sky having become one again
He finally saw that he and the world
Were no longer separate and he had
Reached the place he had always known.

# The Oñate Monument

It's up the road about a mile, the Oñate Center,
With the last Conquistador on his horse about to gallop
Into the moving traffic on the highway.

                              This is just about
As far as he actually had gone according to his historian
Don Juan Perez de Villagra's History, about the way
Don Juan Oñate had come north from Zacatecas
To Christianize the Indians and find the gold
That was not there.
                              Hope drove them, hiding
Their disappointments while changing the names
Of the Pueblos to honor one of their Spanish Saints
Or another. Hispanic adventurers become farmers
With the excuse of converting these Indios and
Even having children by them, married or not
Until they decided it was God's will for them
To stay and they turned Okeh Owingeh into
San Juan de los Caballeros, moving out to build
San Gabriel and then down to what came to be
The Villa Real de la Santa Fe de San Francisco de Asis,
Still the Capital City through 400 tumultuous years
Under one flag or another with as many versions
Of what really went on as to which viejito is talking   ↪

These days a foot of the Conquistador occasionally
Gets cut off by some locals who decide to get even
For what Oñate had done to the Indians down in Acoma
But it gets welded back on and people still grumble
While the Acequia Commission meets and decides
Who gets water and when and the Matachines dancing
While the Church still manages to maintain a sense
That we all belong together in this corner of the world
That still manages to sing in Spring and grow
The corn, the beans and all the fruit that still
Is the treasure of the place in spite of posturing,
And Fiesta Royalties, small time drug deals and
La Hermandad for Heaven's sake.

## Changing The World

*"To cut these trees down is to change the world"* the old
Man said. *"To cut these trees down means the end—*
*"The broken end of three hundred years of growing*
*"Slowly—summer spurt and autumn holding, winter*
*"Dreaming and burgeoning of spring—so slow the*
*"Growth the naked eye will not distinguish rings*
*"When looking at the cut."*

                        The quarter acre being
Cleared counted eighteen piñon among the juniper.
Of these, ten were older than the nation's
History, three had seen the light before the
Pueblos threw the Spaniards back south and out of
Here. In a summer's day on the quarter acre
Reaching up towards the sky, dancing with the
Wind nodding yes and no and touching tenderly
The piñon rustled their farewells.

And now the trees are three cords of wood down
On the ground, stacked four feet tall. No longer
Haven of the raven or the magpie or the finch but
Promise of warmth in winter with the land cleared
And graded for the building yet to come.
*"Yes—the world is changed"* the old man said—

*"The ghosts of those piñon will always be with us,"*
He said, waving his arms slowly turning in the
Small afternoon breeze.

# Midsummer Power Outage

Today the power went out. 3:05 pm.
Yes, we live in the country. With
The Jemez Mountains Electric Co-Op
It happens. No back up. No generator.
Everything went down. Computers.
Phones, yes, only one flush per toilet.

Did not come back on. Hours.
Time does stop, but its summer
Still light, cold herring on black bread
Spoiled rotten, us, not the herring,
Sustenance, all the environmental piety
Does not count for anything. Aware,
Adding up, hearing my father saying
"Live as if you were to die tonight
"But at the same time as if you
"Were to live forever."

The letters not thought out, not
Finished, not written, the debts
Not paid, the answers not given.
Yes, if the power does not get back
We start again to weave a net
To hold it all together, to find
Ways in the daylight to pack up
The few things that can be carried.
To move on, to get to the next one,
The next place to begin again
Feet on the ground, shelter, food, hope
And then the fire, the prayers and all
That makes us human once again.

# The Acequia Commission

The setting is spare. The new Community Center,
Tables, plastic. Chairs, folding. Not the old wood
One would have expected. The Commissioners mostly,
Old, serious. Listening to the new parciante.
The one who had just bought the Quintana place
Asking for clarity, for his water rights according to
The law, "so many acre feet" he said, then
Being told by the Mayordomo, "No, the State Engineer
Does not know. We know."

                              "The law says," the new
Parciante beings. He does not get to finish. "The
"State Engineer's only been here maybe ninety
"Maybe hundred years." A pause. The cougar
Of silence had entered the room.

                                    "We've been
"Here maybe four, five times that. We know. We
"Run things. We say what goes. You want water
"You get it, when we say you get it. This water,
"Is our life, always has been." Murmurs, yessing,
Long silence again. Papers rustle.

                                    The new,
In this one rare case, gives way to the old.

Water, community, agreement, sowing, harvesting.
The old ways. There's a rumble from the cougar
In the back there.  ↳

                    The water comes when they decide.
Los viejos, silent, nodding at each other. Yes, no, yes.
The new ways count, perhaps at County or at
State or the Federales. Here in the bare room
A look, a wave of the hand, a nod then
Everyone there knows. It's time! The Cougar
Gets up and slides out the side door.

And the new one, the one who thought he had rights
When he had bought the old Quintana place
Learns how to be and takes a step to begin
To walk and talk like them, the vecinos
The old ones, the Mayordomo, the Cougar
Out of the Community Center, down to the road
There to look up, down and see the water run.

# Full Moon Equinox at Chaco Canyon

Summer suddenly slides into fulfillment,
The corn ready to be harvested, the grapes
Filled with sugar waiting to be plucked
The apples already blushing and the fields
Proud with the green that they have done.

Next summer's children, all coming into light
In the middle of next year will thank the love
That's made tonight into a balancing of
The years' passing that brought them into being
Enriching all the work that's being done.

The stellar universe through which our small
And troubled planet turns is so immense
It hardly notices how we dance and play
Even though disaster strikes, wars erupt and
Hurricanes invade the dream we still dare to dream.

Building walls of stone to guide the stars,
Discovering ways of catching the bright sun's light
In a magic vault while even the full moon's soft and
Silken glow rises and echoes in constructions made
By the ones that came before, the Ancient ones
Teaching us how to be with each other today.

## The Prize

Those who go looking for it seldom seem to find it.
Those who have their faces and their bodies carved
Into that which they believe will be more attractive
Lose it.
       Those who cannot find it in their own hearts
Never seem to find it in the hearts of others.

                    The wind
Will bring it, sometimes;
 At other times it's the rain or
An unexpected stranger at the door.
              When found
And not recognized it becomes mist and disappears.

Tentative as well as bold, demanding, stubborn as a
Mule can be at times and also generous and even
Forgiving, it lives through tragedy and loss and
Will be there to hold the hand and caress
The old man's hair and touch the child and make
The house bright and the lark sing.
               It will
Even serve to bring clocks to stop and the future
Into a place where it can be shaped — but try
To force it into any canister or box and it flies
Away never to return.
          We all know its habits
And its ways — odd that we rarely seem to know
What to do with it when it decides to come and stay.

## The White Horse

There's a white horse that runs across
The mountain's crest. He's running North
Towards the sky surrounded by the dark
Pines and the distances in which he lives.

That white horse reminds me every day
That it's time to go, to pick up and move,
To let the various pieces of my history find
Themselves and finally pull themselves together.

This winter weather gets wet and fitful and
My place beside the fire is warm and yet
The white horse is up there running, each time
I look up into the mountains, calling me.

# For Love That's Given

When payment of any kind
Is expected by the giver,
It is not love that's given —

Seed planted in receiving earth
Gives all to stalk of wheat,
Apple tree or fir
Without regret —
It gives, and giving all
Fulfills its role.

Ask no return
Of child, of lover
Or even of the busy world.

It comes
When it's not asked, as wind comes,
Or rain, unexpectedly,

And then
Comes back again,
Again.

## The Same Thing

It is the same thing that drives the stallion
To mount the willing mare standing there
In the meadow winking and waving her tail
As if to say "I'm here for you, big boy."

                                    It is
The same thing that drove Mark Anthony and
Caesar to want the power of Empire so as to have
That which each one wanted—

                        The same thing
That drove Henry the Eighth into those paroxysms
Of lust and fury that divided England from Rome—
Always the same down to our time when
Another King of England threw his Empire to the wind
For the whetting of his appetites—

                              We are an odd lot
Inventing grand towering names for that feeling
That comes over us as it came over King David
When he saw Bathsheba bathing on her roof
That summer's afternoon not so long ago
Causing murder and betrayal in the palace.

It's the same thing that's made women careless
And men foolish since it all began, yes, the same
Thing that moves the finches and the other
Birds to build their nests in Spring—that makes
The white tailed doe stand quivering in Autumn
In the high meadows of this mountain range.
The same thing that fuels all the attention given
To the development of abs and quads in health clubs
Across the country and the marketing of creams,
Of clothes, of perfumes and of dreams so as to enhance
The desirability of each and every one of us.

# Are They the Same?

In Spanish
I want you
And
I love you
Use the same words.
Yo te quiero, y
Yo te quiero
Are the same words

In no other language
That I know
Is it put so clearly

And are they really
The same or are they
Equivalent in other
Ways?
       Wanting
And loving — are they
The two sides of the coin?
Or is one a reflection
Of the other?
       Today
And every day I wake
I ask myself to take
Another look to see
Whether they are the same
In Spanish or in any
Other tongue.

# Ten New Mexican Moments

In her eyes, distances;
Wide ones that reach back
Through time as well as place
While at the same time
Defining the future.

Resonance, drumhead speaking
Its many voices, sounds,
Pleasures and urgencies.
To the world it comes now
Its rhythm and sound resound.

Like leaves that change
From the light of first emergence
To the strength of their deep greens
Willing to give back to the sun
Its light and radiance.

Willingness to risk, bravery,
Beauty, the winds, thunder,
All in her eyes as well as
The quiet of the dawn
After a night of dreams.

Once the destination is determined
The course can be set
The stores stowed, the
Rigging checked, the stars
Becoming guides, and one casts off.    ↪

The will to go beyond
Beyond heart, horizon
Or even oceans and stars
Will move the navigator
To care for his companions
Even more than for himself.

Once certain appetites, needs
And even desires have been met
We can then pause
In order to discover heart.
The one that made it possible,
Without which no joy exists.

Hope drives horses, men,
Women and even the stars —
Hope also teaches caution,
Timing, and inquiries are
In order to find the right
Road, Mountain, Home.

All he had learned and done
Brought him to this one
Moment, this place, point
Where the road forks.
It is his heart that chooses
Its future of never before.

Daring was not an issue
Never had been, nor desire.
It was life itself he wanted.
Having seen it in her eyes
He moved quietly to open
The door of what was to be.

## The Two Cousins

Time and love are kin. Both are intangible
And yet touch and shape each and every thing
We do. Each stretches out to distances unseeable
While holding within themselves the power to bunch
Up, creating chaos in their folds as in this piece of
Crumpled paper. Yes, each one envelops all we do
And becomes even more noticeable when either one
Leaves our lives and disappears.

                              When time stops for us, we die.
When love stops we may not die immediately but often
Wish we had.
                    However, when time sings for us and all
Its moves are somersaults of bright delight it's really quite
The same as when we fall in love, head over heels in love,
Heeding the gentle push that nature gives us when we see
A candidate, a likely mate with whom we'd make
A perfect child—and odd how we think it's our free
Will at work when it's only the old wise Mother
Saying, "Yes, that one would do for you"—and then,
There is a time for it, the time that makes it happen, dance,
Sing, and play while one loses all sense of time itself
Discovering the pleasures of forevers and of eternities.
They are indeed kin to each other, these two. They frame
The world in which you and I can be together, so let us
Be sure to love in time so that we may time our love
To be with us in all the hours of our days.

# The Chase

So easy to pursue. It's been bred
In all of us, human or animal,
Even birds are known for it, and
Yet it may not always serve
As well as the waiting game.

We are told of Shiva and the Milkmaids
And the great Eleanor of Aquitaine who
Married and mothered Kings without
Worrying about the details.

                       Songs are
Made out of the waiting and verses
As intricate as medieval embroidery
Can be worked into a fabric whose very
Name is the silk that waits.

                      The chase
And capture disciplines are suited
To the most of us — but then the others,
Those who learn patience and how not
To disturb the leaves, but rather how
To invite attention and desire
Until the world merges into the fire
Of reciprocity to forge the mutuality
Of smiles destined to remain as long
As there are stories to be told.

## In Denver

On Columbus Day, celebrated to remind us all
That it was on that day of discovery that
The rape and pillage of this continent began.

The Sons of Italy parade their pride while
The American Indian Movement moves to join
With those American Italians who decide they'd like
To see the Celebration changed or set aside
Recognizing that "Discovery" became the Law
That would ride astride the taking of lands
Everywhere and anywhere that had not had
The blessing of the Faith or the sacred messages
Of Commerce and Christianity among the Western Arts.

The "abatement" of the Carib Indians as shown
In the log of the Admiral of the Ocean Sea
Clearly pre-dates Bush's "if you're not with us
"You're against us" much as the Crusaders excused
Their devastation of Constantinople.
                                    We are not
Responsible for what may have been done by others
In their time, but are, in fact truly responsible only
For what we do today, as well as for the things
We teach our children and, just having had
A cataract removed from my right eye, perhaps
I see even more clearly that to celebrate the day
The genocide began on this side of the Atlantic
Is not the way to teach history to the children
But perhaps a day that will serve to teach us that
Mistakes may yet have a chance to be corrected
And perspectives to change the way we see the past.

## They Will Say...

"This is the place where he would
"Bring the roses he had cut
"In the garden they had made together,
"The one that overlooked the valley below
"And the pool they would bathe in
"And be together."

           And they will say
"This is the place where he would dress
"The roses and arrange them in the
"Vases they had found together."

And the roses had made their lives
Into a rainbow of color with each petal
Touching another as their fingertips
Would, from time to time, touch each
Other, with love and gentleness,

              And
There will be a few among them who
Will know exactly how much love
Will have gone into those roses on
Rainy Sunday afternoons
In late September.

## To Begin Again

As sun breaks, as gull cries
As fields are tilled
To begin again

As the loved one dies
As hawks wheel
To begin again

As the house burns
And the flood washes away everything
As the friend miscalculates
As bowls break
To begin again
As the direction is lost
And the food runs out
As the orchard is blighted and anger explodes
To begin again

To begin
Each time
Again

From seed to flowering
Without hope of turning
Without prayer
Without rope, without dream  ↳

To begin a long journey without water
Having come a long way across deserts
Having eaten camels

To begin again
Knowing the masquerade is complete
Knowing the sum is false
Knowing your partner betrayed you
Yesterday

To begin again
Each time at dawn
As the wind begins to move
And the fleshing of your bones comes true

Each time
Again

The daffodil grows
The river runs
And you turn

To begin
Again

## On The Path Of Light
### For Rudolfo Anaya

Treading lightly on the path we choose, we
Acknowledge fortune with each step we take.

When we lose our way we drop into the dark.
When we forget ourselves or what
We've learned, we become shadows,
Lacking substance, fragments of that dark.

To have the courage to permit the sun
To bring its clarity into our souls
Is laudable and brilliant. To keep it there
Takes dancing as well as dedication, takes
Laughter as well as that extra distance that
We may have to run along that path.

The dark is necessary, we know, and
There are many that choose that way
Of going, but the trees and rivers,
The stones and mountains, the sky
And clouds are all vibrant in the light.

To be one with the sun
On the side of life
Is not always the easy one.

## That Place

The place we know nothing about,
That place which is the mid point of the Universe
And at the same time the very center of your Heart
That place we know nothing about
Where it all began and where it will end
That place made of hopes, desires and memories,
All the intangible elements that work to shape
Our lives and our mistakes as well as the formations
Of the birds flying South in mid Autumn or
Of the leaves blowing their golden shadows
Around the fields where they scurry
With the pale light of the sun just setting.

That place where heart beats and
Breath moves in and out to make sure
We keep on living in ways that bring
The conscious song to all about us.

                                    That place
Is the only one both magical and tangible
From which we all have come and eventually
Get to while we do the best we can
With all the things given to us.

When we began the journey, having learned
That Greed, Rage and Avarice are the bandits
On the long trip down the road we call
Our lives with some sense of who we are
We hope and trust our teachers
So that we may learn to be with ourselves
In concert with all the others of our kind
In that place.

# Smoke

Only once. That once.
That singular Summer of Love.
That "Candle in the Wind,"
Everything possible and free.

Food, drink and laughter
Songs, dances and delights
Making up the ordered world.
Laughing with each other, smoking
Touching, dancing, loving and being,
Even with the police right there.

Pleased to be the Others
For a change.
        Simple,
Before Aids, Vietnam and
The slippery slope that led
Us into Iraq—
        The hilarious folly
That did not kill thousands
But made for smiles and
Outright loving laughter,
Did happen that summer by the Bay.

"We are all one" Ginsberg said
Without envy, need or power.

Now instead the young are fodder
For the killing fields again and
Even those of us with the best intentions
Are being dragged into supporting terror,
And the bastion of Freedom
Has become the Torturer.

## A Question of Net

Where do we begin?
With Abraham?
Or further back—
At the beginning?

Do I tell my children
That because of the Expulsion
An ancestor left Malaga
For Padua and Venice—
Some say by ship,
Other say on foot up the coast—
And then across the mountains
Always across the mountains,
And across the sea.

Is that the beginning
Of this net?

It always starts
With just a piece of string
A cord to tie us in,
To let us go,
To be, and

There are moments
When we are not the knots,
But the spaces in between
For which there is no name
But which is light.

We know our end
But how do we begin?

## Best To Be Ready

The family icon is a 12th Century Pilgrim shell
With a carving of the "Flight into Egypt" — Joseph
And Mary with the child Jesus on the donkey,
A cherub overhead gentle in its message
Of going for safety, for life, and to this day
There does not seem to be a record of their return.

No stories in the Gospels or the Apocrypha of how
It was they made it back to Nazareth, even
To Jerusalem or even about those years lost
Between the throwing of the money changers out
Of the Temple to the Garden of Gethsemane
Which led to Calvary and the Resurrection.

                                            No
Mention of those years of growing up and going on,
Perhaps to India, some say, inspiring pilgrimages
And other travels around the world.

                            When asked
Why a Sephardic family would have such a shell
To pass on over the generations my Father said
"It's all right, you see, Son, when they went off to Egypt
"There were no Catholics, no Christians, no Protestants.
"They had other things to fight about or to pray to,
"Or for."

            "It's just a reminder to keep on going
"So long as you can and then be sure to tell
"Your children and theirs it's always best to be ready
"To be on the go, moving on," he said.

# Declaration

I am really getting tired of memorial services!
I am ready to try something else.

Has it been the sense of theater
Required by survivors?

I have had practice
For a lot of years tossing ashes,
My father's and some teachers' —
As well as those of a lot of friends.

No one told me I'd grow up to be an ash tosser
And I'd really like to put in
For a different line of work.

Births and marriages
Aren't really my thing anymore
Either
I've done enough of those too.

I'd rather cook for my friends than bury them.

To take up an instrument at my age,
And tone deaf too, won't do.
I'd rather write songs for my friends to sing
And drink and smoke,
And make love and make love,
And make all the stars and planets
Bring their rays
To my love's eyes
To inform her
Of the quantity of light
In the universe without which
There would have been
No life
In the first place
At all.

## Stars Do Move

The Pleiades have shifted and are
No longer in the field of Taurus.

All I've come to learn
Is now reduced to sums
That have to do with banks
Through which no river flows
And not with fields of hope
And meadows of desire.

Young Jesus driving the money men
Out of the Temple knew
Something then that's taken
Me much too long to learn.
                      Trees
Are for birds to build nests in and
To give shelter and bring green
Into the work in Spring and not
Only to be felled and fed into
Sawmills so that they could
Then justify their harvesting.
                       My
Heart aches with the thought
That so much of that which
Begins as flowers turns to dust
And is swept away and so
Often it's only the memory of love
That lasts
Even when stars explode
And the constellations
Change their ways.

## Winter Solstice 1

The Sun stops and stays and rests tomorrow.

The cold up here bites into the bone
We warm ourselves with fire and a smile.
The water in the river still is flowing
Except where it nested in the banks and froze.

No surprise that quiet comes and that we turn
Into the caves and shelters of our lives while
The cold wind blows and we dare to dream.

For so many of us in the Northern half
Of this Planet on which we find ourselves
Turn to faith that Spring will come
While Summer sings its songs down there
In that Southern half of this same world.

Each land enjoys its rituals and beliefs
Each one of which serves us with hope,
With radiance and the love of life.

It is time to turn to the beginning
Once again.

## Winter Solstice II

This Winter Solstice so like all the others
Our kind has weathered since we came
Out of the trees into the savannahs and then
Out into the lands between the rivers where
We became human and learned to till
The ground and plant what we would eat
While also tending to the flocks and beasts
That became domesticated so that we would
Then ride into distances and mysteries
Discovering the spiritual as well as the
World of stars and planets all around us.

And yet, though it is like all the others,
This Winter's staying in the Sun requires us
To be more pensive and concerned and even
Angry that we have permitted ourselves
To become pawns in a game that Powers play
A game that we knew as "Chicken"
When growing up, and learning how to drive
To see how close to come without a crash.  ↳

Now this Winter Solstice could turn itself
Into a disruptive flash shedding its light
So far out into the universe if all, or perhaps
Even a few of those bombs we hold were all
To go off together—and we know this time
Dedicated to the birth of the Prince of Peace
According to some believers—is not a time
To think of the ending of this Planet's spin
Around the Sun and yet we must, before
Our blue planet becomes a used one, like
Mars or one of those other pieces of matter
That bounce about the Universe.

                              We have
Learned to pray, so let us count on doing that
This Christmas Day that Peace may come and stay.

## Tell Me

Tell me
Tell me how precious
Gentleness can be
In a world where violence
Vengeance and victories
Are celebrated.
             Tell me
That there is an awareness
Somewhere in all of us
That will recognize that
Precious element existing
In us all even though
Over run, denied, betrayed,
Still there, the gentleness
That lives in a look,
In a touch, a smile
That reaches out to reassure
To comfort, to be with
In ways that are its own.

Gentle thoughts, hands
And entire beings still
Exist and have a place
In the most violent
Of circumstances,
In any war, national
Or familial.
             Do call
On gentleness before
Disaster strikes.

## To Be Here

When the sun reaches its stopping place having
Gone as far North as it ever does, we all breathe
That sigh that says "It will come back down again!
"It will!"

And then miracles begin to happen, berries turn,
The winter's rabbits move more quickly, the light
Begins to change even though we know we will
Have still more ice and more snow to face.

The year's wheel begins to turn forward again and
Each one of us finds ways to manage and to move
Again toward Spring and its miracles even as we
Turn to deal with the biting cold.

Smoke rises in the slow dark evening air, the deer
Tracks and the coyote's are both elegant in white.
Reasons for loving come again and gentleness
Touches the light of stars.

Hope is born in a manger and oil lamps burn
Beyond their time. The piñon and cedar steady
Their places on the mountain's side and life looks
As if it will come shining again.

I have spent all my life learning to be here this night,
This moment, by this fire, waiting for the future
To come, to bring us all to ourselves first
Then to each other and then to sing.

# The Family Story

Minor priests, associated in the Temple, money lenders,
Bankers, naval officers, traders, architects and poets, nurses,
Builders, cartographers, musicians, and ladies of all kinds,
Brave ones, beautiful, devoted and brainy ones.

A strange lot, buffeted by winds that carried omens,
Somehow always managing to find a donkey, as in the
Past, to get away, or tickets on a ship or plane these days
To carry us from there to here, from danger to a place
Of safety or even temporary rest.

                                    We've always looked
To be on the move, accommodating to the customs of
The place, adapting each time to the strictures that
Made it possible for one generation of our own
To turn into the next.

                              Always this apparent need to
Make a mark, leave an imprint on the sand, build
Bridges, shape water and make a solid out of time.

We are for a moment only, breathing one breath at a time,
Persisting, no matter what it is we do, learning
Each day how to live forever while concurrently
Learning how to die tomorrow at the same time.

## Us

We're not many, counting all of us,
Scattered from here to London and
Down to Sydney too, tied loosely,
More or less connected by Fate and
Phones and by having done all the
Things we did together while sharing
Memories, appropriating myths and
Then going on to manufacture
Our own interpretations
Of being alive.
      Tribal and familial
On one side while wholly singular on
The other, we choose to shape our lives
So as to be involved with those with whom
We share our dreams and dances,
Our bread, our peaches, our thoughts
And our histories.
      One day the children's
Children will say "Oh yes, we know,
"They came from over there, and then
"Were here for a while before they
"Went on" — all the data to be
Stored in computer memories so as
To be accessible in ways undreamed
Before today.
      Every thing that was
Before is here. Touch it. It's us now
And will be them in time.

# Images

Unlike our ancestors who had to rely on words alone
To tell their children of their past adventures we
Now can videotape our lives, photograph our every
Chosen moment and digitize the present so as to
Make it permanent and visible in future years.

There were times when the image of a king
Could be found on coins even when portraits
Were rare, but as painters learned to please,
Not only popes and princes, others wanted
To be memorialized and merchants, along
With bankers, commissioned their own images.

Now we are surrounded by the looks
Of people we have come to know in
Newspapers, on television, on billboards
And find ourselves engaged in conversations
With total strangers in other lands.

Pieces of my own past came to be with me
The other day when my brother asked
If I could find some photographs of him
Growing up to show his daughter since
His own stash had disappeared.

                                             While
Looking through the boxes and the albums
Stowed away for much too long, I found
Yellowed photographs, images of relatives
From almost a century ago and places
That are no longer there today.

                                             Odd
How visual we have become when some of
Those ancestors of ours outlawed even a single
Representation of Jahweh and the human form.

# And I Could Have Been One of Them

The snow fell all night last night. This morning,
Walking through it, the half mile down
The hill to get the Sunday paper and back
Up as the cold mist turned the world
Into black and white like those old photos
Of the war in Russia, I understood in a new way
How it must have been for the boys in that
Division of the Italian Army, green at
16 and 17, sent up to the Russian Front
By Mussolini, at Hitler's demand.
Stalingrad.

Out of the sunbaked hill towns, the groves
Where lemons, oranges and olives came from,
The untrained fodder for the Russian guns
Went, ill-clothed, with gloves so thin that
Fingers froze. The sixty thousand men and
Officers of the Blue Division turned blue
And died — all but eleven hundred and sixty-two,
Who somehow managed to make it through,
And get back to Italy.

Sixty-one years have gone by and it's all
One now, even the memory. Some
Fifty-eight thousand or so may not be so many,
But the stupidity of even one event like that in
The light of the millions dead freezes the heart.

How will I be able to tell my children how stupid
This generation of ours has been and how
Arrogantly this waste keeps on wasting us all away?
In Afghanistan, in Israel, in Florida and in the town
Next door as it did in 'Nam and now Iraq, in
Sierra Leone, Timor and even in the high desert
Where we now live, it still goes on.

## Addressing The Powers

Evoke, bring them on, all of them
Into the light, bring them to us.
Call them, as Ulysses did.
Across the river of blood.
Through the fire —
Make all the right signs.

Sing them on and over — bring
The incantations, the enchantments!
Bring them to us out of the dark
Bring them, fearful and shy,
Sorrowful, weeping as some will be
But bring them to us —
Even the proud ones
The ones still confrontational
The ones that died full of fury
Bitching and swearing still.

Bring them on — even
The long gone poets muttering
In the shade
As well as the sweet ones
The darling ones
Who went ahead, ahead
Of their times, ahead of us.

Sing them to me, softly, slowly,
I need to hear them, to hear them,
To talk to, and with, all of them.

My father and mother
And the twins and all
Those others, friends and dear ones,
All those gone ahead of me.

Bring them,
I need to talk to them
Now.

## Road Poem

To save the soul
The body suffers so much!

All the Jihads, the Holy Wars,
The Massacres — St. Bartholomew's
The Golden Temple, Tehuantepec,
Auschwitz, Bergen-Belsen, the Inquisition,
Athletes in Munich! Soweto!
The Ardeatine caves!
And now Najaf!

Yes, the suicide bombers
Responding out of desperation
With massacres inviting more and
More of the same, begetting violence
Out of violence, in Gaza,
The West Bank and even
On the Temple Mount.

Airplanes blow out of the sky!
All for someone's hope of Heaven!
At the same time
The nurturing of life
Goes on
The gardeners, the nurses!

Somehow gentleness prevails
Even as the fires rage —

The seamlessness of water!

I sit by the road's edge
Fascinated by the power
Of a new green leaf
Forcing its way up
Through the gravel, the concrete —
Through the layering of civilization
Into the light.

# Management

Trust, belief, the possibility made manifest
Otherwise no businesses, no exchange

Each horse trader in a trade believing
He got the best of it — is sure he did

The banker trusted by the depositor trusts
The client who trusts or — no banks

Belief makes the car last and projections
Turn into houses and schools and food

No difference between the thieves' market in Morocco
And other exchanges in New York, Tokyo, and London

Break the trust, lie, dissemble, disinform
And disaster comes surging with no surprise

In Genesis the first three stories are
Disobedience, disobedience and fratricide

Still we learn to be with one another
In spite of disappointments, unbelief

You can only find it when it comes looking for you
You can only sing it when you become the song

Comfort comes when you've stopped trying and
Ease appears when the Way finds you out

Flowers bloom and trees touch sky
The earth draws the sun, angels sail on,
And the air enchants the petals of the rose

## Bon Appetit

Controlled by our appetites, not differing so much from the horses
Down in the pasture by the river, we remember we were prey once
Instead of the predators we've become.We go from meal to meal,
Doing all the daily that needs doing in order to feed ourselves, to
Feed the children and eventually all those out there that need our
Help, our hands, our hearts.

We build freeways, bridges and cathedrals.We design and launch
Ships that take us up as far as and beyond the moon and build
Engines of destruction that can and may yet undo the work of aeons
Of evolution and the quest for good.We find ways of making up to
Each other once there's been a war, a fight — even a divorce — and we
Find it appropriate to work it out for the greater good — but for some
Of us it's still impossible to break bread together without calling up
All the curses that our ancestors hurled at each other.

We eat, we gain and lose weight, look at starving children on the
Telly without missing even one quick bite.We drink what's out there
And advertised so that we too may look like the Prince or Princess of
The moment.We send food with our good wishes to celebrate a tribal
Rite and occasionally, suffering from an attack of Guilt, we go down
To the kitchen where the homeless come to feed and ladle out the
Spoonfuls of that which is too much for us, still controlled by our
Appetites.

We raise our glasses to toast a victory, our way of counting coup.We
Remember friends no longer with us, we even find religious solace
Eating the body and the blood of God in rituals celebrated around
The world.We eat and, in between the eating, we manage to find
Time to dream, to make love and have the children that we'll teach to
Sow and plant and reap so that they too will have enough to eat and
To share with friends while dreams are relegated to those moments
In between our meals, or between the phone calls that will tell us
Whether there's enough that's been put away to keep us safe,
Well-fed and happy for a time.

## Losing Friends

You said we lost three friends last month,
As if we had misplaced them, or left one on
The seat in the train, another in the market
And the third behind the shelves marked "Fiction"
At the bookstore near the Plaza.

There are things
As well as people that, once lost, can not
Be found again or replaced.

The euphemism of
Loss, instead of death, auspicious in its use
To hide the inauspicious fact that these three
Friends will only continue to exist as thoughts
Or memories, so long as we keep them in
Our minds, or as we may choose to shape
A phrase, thinking of them, that we would shape
In a different way because of them.

They will continue
To be with us, which is why so many of us are bent
To prayer, memorializing those who have gone
Before us, lost, wandering in the dark, making us
Think again of what we did not say to them, all
That we should have said or done with them
We did not do.
Missing them.

# Wanting Something After We Die

I suppose that most of us do, in fact
Want something after we die.

Saving our souls will get some of us to heaven,
Those of us who are fortunate enough to believe,
And organized religion has worked that one for a while.

Others work furiously at their art knowing
That steel and paint will last longer than their hands or eyes
Thus giving them immortality of another kind;
Kin perhaps to the one that moved ancestors to
Paint bison, deer and other strong shapes on cavern walls in Spain,
In Africa and even here in this high desert land.

                                    And then there were
Ramses and Cheops building their pyramids,
Launching pads to the sky.

                       These days we hear
News of men who kill themselves so as to kill their enemies,
Assuring entry into future palaces and places in
Their heavens for ever after.

                       Those others who are
Themselves immortalized as future statues,
Or on postage stamps, or even as names on the spines of books
In libraries or as data encrypted on discs or in the smiles
Of their children's children, all seem to be devoted to it.

And yet,
I know what matters
Is the doing,
Nothing
Else.

## What Is Your Name?

Who are you,
Saint of the near miss, the close call?
Turning the car's wheel
Deflecting the knife's point
So that we walk out of the hospital
The next day greeting the sun
Gratefully?

What are you, guardian angel,
Kachina, invisible spirit and friend,
You—the one who makes the judge
Hear our side of the case, who drops
The name from the list,
Wakes the lookout on time
And makes one miss the train
That connected with the plane that goes down?

I build you this poem at dawn
Gratefully listening to the squawking of jays,
To the sound of water falling
And to the intermittent silence
Wondering how it is that so few
Know you, acknowledge you, praise you,
Saint of the near miss, the close call.

# Yes — suddenly, it's green!

The valley down below, overnight,
It seems, turned green, the leaves,
Hesitant and tender, began to tint
The air the other day, but
This morning, out they came
Brightening the air, announcing Spring!

The red breasted finch calls from
The piñon's topmost branch, another one
Responds and they fly off together
Into the air which has turned
Brighter than it has been.

                             Yes, it's green!
The cottonwoods down by the river
Are no longer grey, the elms
No longer etched against the sky —
As if pen and ink had drawn them
Stiffly in the air —

                  Suddenly
It's green again and time to wonder how
It is the trees, the grasses and
The hills know to come out green again
At this same blessed time, just when we had
Almost given up the hope that brought us here.

## We All Want

To believe once more, to know with absolute
Certainty, to discover the Secret of it all again,
To be sure.

        We all want that, particularly
When one hears that this friend has died and
That one is so damaged by his life he might
As well be dead or that other one, the one
Who was the best man at your wedding
Cannot see well enough to move around.

We all want to believe that we can in fact
Believe just once again that when the Gods
Were young and Europa went dancing with
That Bull and Titian and all the other famous
Painters invented versions of the same old stories.

They were true then because we,
Like the stories, are getting old as well;
And true belief is given only to those
Whose youth has not yet been burned
Into a crisp and hope is still willing to
Come around at dawn.

        We all want
That which is around the corner and stare
Amazed at those remaining few of us who can
Still put their faith into the far away,
The ephemeral, the unseen,
The yet to be proven, the unfounded
While keeping smiles and hopes and wants
In check, listening to tomorrow
Sing its constant song.

## The Way Things Are

This was once a country for the young
As old Yeats filled with watery wisdom
Used to say and it still is, since there is hardly
Any room for anything but youth
In its marketing equations.

Live and drive at your best rate
Is what we're told to do and want
For as long as body's obsolescence
Will permit and appetites remain.

The consequences will all take care of
Their own selves, the way Afghanis, Iraqis
And Palestinians all have learned to do.

Doomed to reinvent disaster each day
All of us caught in the net of greed pretend that
This is just the way things are supposed to be.

Not good enough, some say, there must be change
Before we all go away and disappear
As the dinosaurs did the other day.

# The Business of Poetry

The business of poetry
    is more than the arrangement of readings, the
    trading of favors, the wooing of audiences, or
    the management of notices, of schedules and
    publications.

The business of poetry
    is more than the evocation of feelings, the
    confrontation of falsehoods, the creation of
    visions of order and the promise of bountiful
    pleasures.

The business of poetry
    is more than a transaction for dinner, or
    solace, or recognition or even of vengeance.

The business of poetry
    is more than an advertisement for love
    discovered, uncovered, appreciated or lost.

The business of poetry
    is the recognition of that which is true, which
    brings us face to face with ourselves in the
    morning and with laughter at noon.

The business of poetry
    is the flight of the kestrel, the throat of the
    jaguar and the sound of a frozen river
    breaking to run in the spring.

It is the recognition of the child by the father
    and the song of the mother at evening.

It is that which makes the heart glad, the
    harvest bountiful and permits hope to
    rise up once more in the throat of the weary.

The business of poetry is poetry.

# The Making of Poetry

## I.

"Why do you write?" "What made you decide?"
"Why do you persist?" "How did you get started?"
"What drove you to it?" "Does it ever pay?"

The poet is seen as someone strange,
An apparition, of no earthly use,
Someone who hears voices, sees visions,
Feels tremors caused by battles fought
Between armies of the day
And armies of the night.

Perhaps that's why
So many of us decide to hide in academies
Playing the roles of teachers to the young,
Hoping to eat and not be noticed
While doing the work necessary as blood,
Indispensable as water.

There are certain kinds of glues that hold broken
Toys together, or bits of a glass bowl, or lives —
Glues that become transparent
When they harden to hold things together.

Perhaps that is all that poetry is —
A way of fixing what breaks,
A way of invisibly mending what's not right,
A way of saying "Yes" — to all questions.

Perhaps also a way of answering each other
In ways that will not wound or kill. ⮑

## II.

We deal in surprises. Our magic
Turns words into delights or to tears.
We remind, recall and represent.

With us, complaints become eloquence
And when anger is vented by us even
Revolutions can be fired up by
What we do.
                    Lonely and alone even
While dancing or whipping up a crowd
We give people reasons to fall in love,
To rediscover the universe, to learn
About hope in winter — and even
To believe in themselves.

Our own experiences become mirrors
For all those who read and hear
Our work.

                              Older than
Iron mongers we are those whose
Craft was learned in caves even
Before the great temples were
Raised to honor Ishtar and Isis
And all the other early Gods

We praise Orion and sing for
The Seven Sisters remembering
To see even when blinded and
To hear even when we are deaf
So that we may be voice
And vanguard for all that happens here. ↪

## III.

Yes, they say we use empty words
They say "Your words are empty,
They do not hold a thing. It's only
Living flesh that counts — the unique person
Standing there in front of you." And yet

All of us are interchangeable,
Queen Isabella's skull and Montezuma's
Look mightily the same today
And all the world's magnificence
Fades into gray as we go on.

It is not bone and muscle that remain,
Not tongue, not brain, but words alone
That sing and come back again with
Tears and joy and pride and tenderness
To shine and shape our days.

We are blessed with  voices; let us then
Praise it all, even the pain, the bad choices
And the falling rain; praising fish
And birds and children out at play
Know that our empty words are still
And will always remain
The only keepers of our dreams and histories.

## Another Way of Looking at It

In the second grade the six year old girl
Asks Miss Sandoval, "What is War?"
"Where is it?" "What do they mean
"When they say they're going to War?"
"Where is that place?"

Miss Sandoval replies
"It's where people fight and kill each other,
"When countries argue and can't agree and where
"One country or a group wants to control another,
"They fight, they go to War."

"Like a whole country
"Can get drunk and angry or jealous like Paco's uncle
"Gets when he gets drunk and gets into a fight?"
The girl asked.

"No, not like that" the teacher said
"But come to think of it, you may be right."

# For Mark

There are some who build great bridges
Say London, or Avignon or the Golden Gate
Tying one shore to another, and there are others
Who build tall arrows to pierce the sky like Eiffel
Or even shape it, like Gehry or Jorn Utzøn
Who built the Opera House in Sydney
But my brother Mark with his sculptures
That dance in the air like giant cranes
About to take flight and soar into the world
Of imagination, become magicians themselves
Turning perspective on its head and perception
Into a series of surprises.

                    Large or small
Each one elects to speak to its viewer in
A language of its own and the conversation
That ensues usually brings smiles, delight
And an appreciation that space and air
And light can be created out of heavy steel
Or weighty wood to dance in the viewer's eye,
Not only in the moment when the sculpture
First becomes part of the viewer's life, but
For all the time to come in which steel,
Space and gravity and balance engage
With memory and perception to dance today
And into the future in ways beyond our lives.

## No Matter the Time

No matter the time, the place or the position of the stars.

Ninety one she was, blind, weighing less than a feather
In the arms of her quadraplegic son's friend who had
Come to carry her up to be bathed. "Hold me" she said
The day before she died.

No matter the time, the place or the position of the stars.

Young father so proud of her, his wife, mother now,
With the baby, having been seen to be perfect, nursed,
Warmed, cuddled finally to sleep, she, wife, mother looked
Up at him, tired, with tears in her eyes, so pleased,
Reaching for his hand saying "Hold me."

No matter the time, the place or the position of the stars.

The three year old on the beach having just kicked the
Large many colored ball across the sand into the water
For the very first time, applauded by his father, so pleased,
Runs up, jumping into his arms laughing and shouting
Saying "Hold me."

No matter the time, the place or the position of the stars.

The sixteen year old sailor on his first trip out, North
Atlantic run, when the ship was hit, found himself
In the dark cold water, hanging on to a hatch cover,
So cold, wet, alone, seeing nothing but the crests
Of the waves. November dark freezing already when
Two shapes appeared looking like angels leaning
Towards him as he let go into the dark cold
Saying "Hold me."  ⤳

No matter the time, the place or the position of the stars.

       The two of them having
Heard of each other from friends, met after Christmas,
Discovering not only winter but spring and summer and
The entire universe in each other that night and waking,
Said each to the other with one voice "Hold me."

No matter the time, the place or the position of the stars.

       The lover leaving
With no reason except that the time had
Come, after so many years, to go, to be other than
What had been between them saying to the beloved
That last morning, "Hold me."

No matter the time, the place or the position of the stars.

The sergeant, in Fallujah, while being carried by two
Of his men to the van that had been ambushed,
With his guts mixed in with his belt, its buckle,
The shreds of his camouflage jacket all mixed up
In the shit and blood running out of his lap
Looking up to Tim on his right, saying "Hold me."

No matter the time, the place or the position of the stars.

Each day holding, each day letting go, everywhere
Each one of us having come or gone, believing it to count
Or not, each one hoping, waiting, leaving, loving as if
There were no time at all except the moment, holding
And letting go while the stars stand still.

## For Barbara and Casa Girasol

Some say it's luck, others choose
To thank the stars.

Our story is we had the chance to flee
Into Egypt, then to Spain, Italy and China,
And then to this valley green in Spring with
Flowering trees while up in the mountains fires
Continue to burn their savage oranges and reds.

At dawn the blue gray haze from the Borrego fire
Is not that different from the one enveloping
Bethlehem and Jenin. It makes our eyes burn
While hope and light turn into day again. It's
Not only greed and lies and wars that work to
Divide us; inattention and bad manners also
Conspire to separate us from what we need.

Love and care have built this house.May it stand
To remind all of us that in spite of apparent
Impossibilities, attention and the grace of being well
With one another still work to build things that will
Make smiles happen long after all of us are gone.

## Easy Now

Easy now, we've built a house again,
Perhaps it's time to move.
                              How is it
That as soon as permanence appears
The old familial sense of moving on makes
Itself manifest.

                    The rest of time, our time,
Means so many more things today since
This aspect of the work's been done and we can
Now go on just like the journeyman carpenter
Out of Bethlehem to Egypt and from there
To Spain, to Italy, to China and to Peru,
Stopping, to restore breath and provisions
In this valley where four hundred years ago
Oñate and his crew stopped to establish
A New Kingdom that would endure "for
"All time to come" and since then, the
Tides of conquest move out and back
And nothing lasts, stone crumbles and
Books disappear.

                    We turn to look.

The river in this valley runs its way for all
That which is yet to come without thinking of
You or me or wars or presidents but only
Of the air and clouds and birds and sun.

And another friend has died and gone,
And yes, perhaps, it is time
To move and to go on.

# Tell Us

What is it about us that needs to create enemies?
In the old days it was Satan. He who
Had been Lucifer, the Maker of Light,
Who would seduce the girls, the pure ones,
Turn them into witches who rode broomsticks
Because they felt so good under their skirts.

The Auto da Fe's of the Inquisition, the trials at Salem,
All the illusions that generate killing sprees
From the barbecuing of Joan of Arc
To the Weapons of Mass Destruction,
The creation of today's Republic of Fear
Is only another stop on the highway
Known as the "Management of Illusions."

The killing of Jews, the enslavement of Blacks,
The oppression of those already oppressed make
For bad examples in the bringing up of children.

What is it about us that needs to be cruel?
Always in the name of another illusion!
It is written that it was Eve's sin and
Adam's concurrence that started the troubles.

A new book should be written with grace
And with friendship that would acknowledge
The past as another mistake to be undone.

Perhaps it should be written by birds
Who have learned to fly together, in order, over
Great distances, always in line with each other
Defining horizons in ways that are clear
Leaving no room for vengeance or torture.

Is it Greed? Is it Need? Is it Fear?

Tell us!
We need to know.

## Enemy Combatants

Sitting at the table, the TV on
With news of Kandahar,
The Taliban, retired generals'
Hired faces spouting, telling—
And now the Inmates
In Guantanamo's stockade not
Prisoners of War, in spite of
The fact we are at War
Or are we?

Convenience dictates
What we're supposed to think.

"The topography in Afghanistan
Is much like the one here" I am told.

Windy, cold winter mornings,
Long nights, dark
And ice, all of us under
The same sky, at night,
The same constellations,
Jupiter coming to court the Moon.

I am dismayed that we
Have not learned, learned
How to be at peace with one
Another, not in Gaza,
Nor Zimbabwe, Uzbekistan.
Kirgistan or any other Stan,
Or even Chimayo, not far from here.

The sons of Isaac and
The sons of Ishmael still
At each other's throats.

## *Once Again*

This cold Sunday afternoon
Filled with the clarity of the New Year
Dancing light and hope together
While mixing bits and pieces
Of last year's failures
Rising to be remembered before
They all drop down to be stowed
Away for the balance of the voyage.

Expectations unfulfilled, work wasted,
The bite of disappointment, promises
Unkept, all come to be acknowledged
As the late afternoon breeze lengthens
Shadows and the former black stallion,
Gelded just last week, stands
Expectantly at the pasture's edge
Eyeing the mares continuously, not
Aware that he is no longer there
For them and then, down by the pond,  ↪

The intrepid cat caught by the ice
And drowned as the surface gave way,
Still lies there frozen where he had
Pounced on his prey head down
Collared by his fate and the cold.

While the death of one of us last
Summer underlines once more the
Fact that tomorrow is not ever
Promised to or by any one, and
We know that we must find a way
To come to hope again, to learn
Once more to trust and to believe
That in spite of winter's bite
Soft spring will come once more.

Each turn in its time
Changes things around
And a blue black crow caws
Life into the bare branches.

## War Once More

Tonight's the Equinox, it will make it easy to remember
This night as the one in which the bombs first rained down
On Baghdad so long ago.
                              War once more,
And this time without a cause, except the one of greed.
Dealing with a dictator and then, when he refused to play,
The need to go after him, trumpeting the eradication
Of the bad while doing worse.

                              Yes, go back to the beach in front of Troy
Where Achilles, Hector and Gods and Goddesses all joined
In the fight because Honor had been breached,
Helen taken, loyalties engaged and great acts
Of bravery imprinted in our collective consciousness for
These last four thousand years.
Today in spite of failed attempts
To make this war a war of honor,
To liberate an entire people from cruelty, we stand indicted
By a world that sees us as the giant Hypocrite among nations.

The Planet spins its course around the Sun and we are still
Amazed at how much we've learned about this Earth while we
Continue to behave in ways that could have been discarded some
Centuries ago if we truly had grown in wisdom and in grace,
While remembering this night as the one in which the bombs
First rained down on Baghdad so long ago.

                              War once more.

No other species evolving on this planet has ever been
As cruel to its kind as we have proven ourselves to be.
Lions and baboons, horned goats and bison will, at rutting time,
Demand and fight for more access and impregnation rights
So as to insure the propagation of a particular strain of seed.  ↳

Horses, Canadian geese and even magpies proceed
With eager dances to impress potential mates; but they do so without
Destroying their own kind.

We are the only ones who do so.

                    War once more;
And the tragedy turns on the fact that
We're made to forget Kosovo, Chechnya, Tibet, the Philippines, Angola,
And Haiti and Colombia where we're doing once again
What we did in Chile, in Guatemala, and not so long ago
In the lands of the Iroquois, the Comanche, the Maya,
And all the other Indian Nations of this hemisphere.

The same thing done by Genghis Khan and his Golden Horde.
In a different time and place.
                    War once more
And we are letting ourselves be told that
The cause is right as so many in the past were told—
The Germans told by Hitler,
The Arabs told by Suleiman, the Spaniards by Cortez
And by Pizarro, and the English by one King Henry or another,
And even today, the Israelis by Sharon.

                    This Spring still
Manages to bring the color green out of the pastures
And out of the dark branches of the trees.

It continues its immemorial functions of renewal not only in the landscape
But even in the hearts of those who still have the will to hope
That change is possible and that in time our children will have come
To learn that human talents can be directed
To the building of a road that will lead us to a place of grace
Where food and shelter and music and the dance
Can be shared by all who know that war once more
Is not ever to be waged again.

## For Frank Waters *June 9, 1995*

Beat of wings — the eagle has flown from the peak.
Quiet times — easy — the hunter has gone beyond.
The one who opened the way for us to seek,
To learn, to uncover and to know, is gone.
Our guide has gone to his rest.

For so long he taught us all with his way of knowing,
Made it all come to life, the river's courses,
The sacred mountains, and all the different ways
Of being part of the spirit world; he knew.
Our guide has gone to his rest.

We can see his eye still fixed on the far horizon line
Beyond which all the secrets are hidden, the ones
He would find to bring to us. He taught us it was
All one. The deer, the hunter, the lake, the sky.
Our guide has gone to his rest.

Seeker and Teacher, Seer and Friend, touching it all.
Busy writing it down for our children's children in time
And for us — our world better because of him — our
Time, our lives and our understanding better as well.
Our guide has gone to his rest.

Yes — it is a mournful Spring for us. He is gone!
But how much more joyful because he was here!

# Everywhere

Hawk on the hill, golden in dawn light, taste of mint,
    starfire and solstice,
Woman at the door, trembling, with a butcher knife
    held hard in her hand,
Twin colts, dark, weanlings, butting and dancing in
    the snow in the meadow,
Back hoe, grunting, charging, digging, dumping to carve
    a foundation for the new house,
The trillions of stars and poetry everywhere.

Shapes of steam rising into cold air becoming instant
    calligraphy,
Surgeon's fingers, latex gloved in the hard light racing to cut,
    to piece, to sew life back to life,
Father with his sons under the hood of the car
    learning and teaching,
Apples and pears, grapes, chiles and corn in neighboring
    baskets at the Farmer's Market,
The conscious cruelty of men and poetry everywhere.

Long shadows across the barrancas, distant mountains
    like torn strips of paper, purple and gray;
Other shades of gray shimmering in the feathers of doves
    cooing and curling in the barn;
Old, gnarled, life stained hands reaching down through
    the floor into the holy mud at the Santuario,
Other hands, hands of young lovers, touching, not touching,
    teasing, touching, not touching and touching,
The smile in a newborn's eye and poetry everywhere.

If not seen in the light or the dark and if not heard
In the sound of the wind or in the chirping of nest building birds,
Or perceived as the smell of rain or the baking of bread
Each day's glory turns into stale ashes in spite of the fact
That it's always there, and everywhere — poetry.

# The Gulls Still Soaring
## For Stewart Udall

It was that first summer sixty nine years ago
When we had just arrived to find refuge in California.
I had just turned fourteen, not yet fully aware of
How close we had come to not making it, not really
Understanding how good fortune and our parents' planning
Had made it possible for us to get away into a future
That gave us our lives instead of having to be sent
Back to Italy to break rocks and the death camps.

Yes it was that first summer at the seashore
At Point Reyes, at Drake's Bay, with the gulls wheeling
Their freedom in the air that made us all feel
That the beaches, the surf, the sky, the air itself
Were all part of that freedom that we had been
Fortunate enough to come to and to share.

Then, so many years later, after the War,
After having sailed out into that not so pacific
Pacific Ocean and grown up as a merchant seaman
Sailing out to 'canal and up to New Guinea and
Then North to Biak, to Leyte and Lingayen and
Back to the America that had given us our lives
Time, circumstances and the fates worked
So many years later to have given me the privilege
Of meeting that man, that giant among men
Stewart Udall, who, with his vision, his heart
And his devotion to all that is good for all of us
Had turned that Point Reyes beach into the first of those
Heritage areas that now stretch from Georgia
To Maine and from Washington to Florida.

This Visionary, inventing a conscience for America
To preserve the land in its beauty, to fight
Against the continuing spoilage of the waste      ⤷

Generated by the Atomic Age, begining
A new awareness of our true responsibilities
To those Nations who had been here before us,
This teacher and diplomat who served all
Of us is now gone to join the gulls still soaring
Above Drake's Bay, the Canada Geese flying
Back North above our heads this Spring,
Gone, after having fathered an aggregate of children
Whose sense of responsibility to the places where we live
And to how we are with each other has made them
Want to serve as he did in all the years of his working life
To make sure that all of us leave each place we live in
Better when we leave than it was when we arrived.

A long way from that first summer in America for me
To this Spring time in the evening of my own life
Thankful that Fate conspired once more to grant
Me a boon, that of meeting that Visionary,
Teacher and most generous and wise philosopher
Who married foresight and practicality to make
This world a better place when he left it than
It had been when he first came into it, those
Ninety years ago when the gulls were wheeling
As they will be flying, still, unless, because of our own
Stupidity we cause this whole world to crash
Into the nothingness that our atomic age is
Fully capable of causing.
                              For having been here, we,
All of us who knew him, give thanks and praise.

## Inland

Here, inland, so far from the sea
The sound of Jeffers, of Everson,
Of Homer, Dante and Columbus
And all those other Seafarers is muted.

The north wind comes and
I know it to be the same wind and storm,
The same sky and stars, the same dream
That savages my nights, those I endured
When I lived there —
Out on the Pacific Ocean's edge,
But Memory still serves
As it brings back the planting
Of the trees I put into the sandy soil
At Stinson, wondering how they stand today.

Years later now, not having changed that much,
I still find myself putting trees into the land
Where I am now, curious once again as to how
They will be when I will have become ash
Or, rotting in the ground, find some way
To have what will have become of me
Serve them, those trees I planted,
The ones on the Coast, the ones here,
In the high desert serving birds and beetles
Until it's time for them to die.

# The Cliff's Edge

Sitting here downwind from Los Alamos
Where they are still building PITS
As if there were not enough missiles,
And nuclear warheads deployed
On the fourteen Trident submarines
And on the launching pads across
This world of ours to incinerate and
To end history even more absolutely
Than the dinosaurs were eliminated
Those aeons ago.

               Tonight I am angry
That so many of us continue to ignore
What has been done in the name of Peace
And Security to bring us all to the edge
The very edge of the cliff of disappearance.

Speaking to the spirits, inventing a variety
Of Gods to be obeyed,  adored, revered
And served, to come to know Love
And all the delights we humans
Have known to put together, histories,
Achievements and then to become again
Aware that all of it from Zeus to Allah
From Buddha to the Christ we all
Are one finger's touch on one button
To be launched into Eternity as if
We had never been here at all

We are at the cliff's edge and stop
We must before one politician
Or another decides to bring all
Humankind into a crust of ash.

## Ordering Information

*Call your order to* 505–982–0066
*or fax it to* 505–982–6858

*or write to*
*PENNYWHISTLE PRESS*
PO Box 734
Tesuque, New Mexico 87574

*e-mail:* pennywhistle@newmexico.com
*website:* www.pennywhistlepress.com

16663580R10067

Made in the USA
San Bernardino, CA
13 November 2014